AGATHA CHRISTIE biography bio book

by David Right

ALL COPYRIGHTS RESERVED 2017

Copyright 2017 by David Right - All rights reserved.

This document is geared towards providing exact and reliable information in regards to the topic and issue covered. The publication is sold with the idea that the publisher is not required to render accounting, officially permitted, or otherwise, qualified services. If advice is necessary, legal or professional, a practiced individual in the profession should be ordered.

- From a Declaration of Principles which was accepted and approved equally by a Committee of the American Bar Association and a Committee of Publishers and Associations.

In no way is it legal to reproduce, duplicate, or transmit any part of this document in either electronic means or in printed format. Recording of this publication is strictly prohibited and any storage of this document is not allowed unless with written permission from the publisher. All rights reserved.

The information provided herein is stated to be truthful and consistent, in that any liability, in terms of inattention or otherwise, by any usage or abuse of any policies, processes, or directions contained within is the solitary and utter responsibility of the recipient reader. Under no circumstances will any legal responsibility or blame be held against the publisher for any reparation, damages, or monetary loss due to the information herein, either directly or indirectly.

Respective authors own all copyrights not held by the publisher.

The information herein is offered for informational purposes solely, and is universal as so. The presentation of the information is without contract or any type of guarantee assurance.

The trademarks that are used are without any consent, and the publication of the trademark is without permission or backing by the trademark owner. All trademarks and brands within this book are for clarifying purposes only and are the owned by the owners themselves, not affiliated with this document.

PREFACE

Agatha Christie also wrote romance novels under the pseudonym Mary Westmacott, and was occasionally published under the name Agatha Christie Mallowan.

Agatha Christie is the best-selling author of all time. She wrote eighty crime novels and story collections, fourteen plays, and several other books. Her books have sold roughly four billion copies and have been translated into 45 languages. She is the creator of the two most enduring figures in crime literature-Hercule Poirot and Miss Jane Marple- and author of The Mousetrap, the longest-running play in the history of modern theatre.

Agatha Mary Clarissa Miller was born in Torquay, Devon, England, U.K.

Table of Contents

ALL COPYRIGHTS RESERVED 2017 2

PREFACE 4

CHAPTER 1- THE BIOGRAPHY OF AGATHA CHRISTIE 7

    Synopsis 7

    Background 7

    Fame and Tumult 8

    Cast of Characters 8

    A mysterious breakdown 9

    Sold More Than Two Billion Copies 10

CHAPTER 2- AGATHA CHRISTIE MARRIAGE AND LATER LIFE 11

    The Pale Horse 12

    Agatha Christie and Torquay 14

CHAPTER 3- THE DISAPPEARANCE OF AGATHA CHRISTIE 16

CHAPTER 4- BEST AGATHA CHRISTIE BOOKS 23

    The ABC Murders (1936) 23

    A Murder Is Announced (1950) 24

    And Then There Were None (1939) 24

    Curtain: Poirot's Last Case (1975) 24

    Death on the Nile (1937) 25

    Murder On The Orient Express (1934) 25

    The Murder at the Vicarage (1930) 26

    The Murder of Roger Ackroyd (1926) 26

    The Mysterious Affair at Styles (1920) 27

    One, Two, Buckle My Shoe (1940) 27

CHAPTER 5- INTERESTING FACTS ABOUT CHRISTIE'S LIFE 30

    11 Reasons Agatha Christie Was as Interesting as Her Characters 30

CHAPTER 6- CHRISTIE AGATHA WRITING SKILLS AND STYLES 34

    What made Agatha Christie's stories stand out?..34

    The Mysterious Affair at Styles by Agatha Christie......................................35

    What was Agatha good at?..35

    And Then There Were None by Agatha Christie 36

    Agatha christie Quotes on writing...40

    About Hercule Poirot 42

        A Great Man..43

        The Mystery of the Blue Train 43

        Playing Poirot..44

        Friends and Partners..45

CONCLUSION 46

CHAPTER 1- THE BIOGRAPHY OF AGATHA CHRISTIE

Agatha Christie was a mystery writer who was one of the world's top-selling authors with works like Murder on the Orient Express and The Mystery of the Blue Train.

"People often ask me what made me take up writing ... I found myself making up stories and acting the different parts. There's nothing like boredom to make you write. So by the time I was 16 or 17, I'd written quite a number of short stories and one long, dreary novel. By the time I was 21, I finished the first book of mine ever to be published."

—Agatha Christie

Synopsis

Born on September 15, 1890, in Torquay, England, Agatha Christie published her first novel, The Mysterious Affair at Styles, in 1920, and went on to become one of the most famous writers in history, with mysteries like Murder at the Vicarage, Partners in Crime and Sad Cypress. She sold billions of copies of her work, and was also a noted playwright and romance author. She died on January 12, 1976.

Background

Best-selling author Agatha Christie was born Agatha Mary Clarissa Miller on September 15, 1890, in Torquay, Devon, in the southwest part of England. The youngest of three siblings, she was educated at home by her mother, who encouraged her daughter to write. As a child, Christie enjoyed fantasy play and creating characters, and, when she was 16, moved to Paris for a time to study vocals and piano.

In 1914, she wed Colonel Archibald Christie, a Royal Flying Corps pilot, and took up nursing during World War I. She published her first book, The Mysterious Affair at Styles, in 1920; the story focused on the murder of a rich heiress and introduced readers to one of Christie's most famous characters—Belgian detective Hercule Poirot.

Fame and Tumult

In 1926, Christie released The Murder of Roger Ackroyd, a hit which was later marked as a genre classic and one of the author's all-time favorites. She dealt with tumult that same year, however, as her mother died and her husband revealed that he was in a relationship with another woman. Traumatized by the revelation, Christie disappeared only to be discovered by authorities several days later at a Harrogate hotel, registered under the name of her husband's mistress.

Christie would recover, with her and Archibald divorcing in 1928. In 1930, she married archaeology professor Max Mallowan, with whom she traveled on several expeditions, later recounting her trips in the 1946 memoir Come, Tell Me How You Live. The year of her new nuptials also saw the release of Murder at the Vicarage, which became another classic and introduced readers to Miss Jane Marple, an enquiring village lady.

Cast of Characters

Poirot and Marple are Christie's most well-known detectives, with the two featured in dozens of novels and short stories. Poirot made the most appearances in Christie's work in titles that included Ackroyd, The Mystery of the Blue Train (1928) and Death in the Clouds (1935). Miss Marple has been featured in books like The Moving Finger (1942) and A Pocket Full of Rye (1953), and been played on screen by actresses like Angela Lansbury, Helen Hayes and Geraldine McEwan. Other notable Christie characters include Tuppence and Tommy Beresford, Colonel Race, Parker Pyne and Ariadne Oliver.

A mysterious breakdown

The year 1926 was an important one for Christie. It saw the publication of her first hugely successful novel, The Murder of Roger Ackroyd, in which the narrator (the character in whose voice the story is told) is the murderer. It was also a year of personal tragedy. Christie's mother died in 1926 and Christie discovered that her husband was in love with another woman. She suffered a mental breakdown and on December 6 she disappeared from her home, and her car was found abandoned in a quarry. Ten days later, acting on a tip, police found her in a hotel in Harrogate, England, where she had been staying the entire time, registered under the name of the woman with whom her husband was having his affair. Christie claimed to have had amnesia (severe memory loss), and the case was not pursued further. She divorced her first husband two years later.

In 1930 Christie married Sir Max Mallowan, a leading British archaeologist. She often accompanied him on his expeditions in Iraq and Syria and placed some of her novels in those countries. In Come, Tell Me

How You Live (1946) she wrote a humorous account of some of her travels with her husband.

Sold More Than Two Billion Copies

Writing well into her later years, Christie wrote more than 70 detective novels as well as short fiction. Though she also wrote romance novels like Unfinished Portrait (1934) and A Daughter's a Daughter (1952) under the name Mary Westmacott, Christie's success as an author of sleuth stories has earned her titles like the "Queen of Crime" and the "Queen of Mystery." Christie can also be considered a queen of all publishing genres as she is one of the top-selling authors in history, with her combined works selling more than 2 billion copies worldwide.

Christie was a renowned playwright as well, with works like The Hollow (1951) and Verdict (1958). Her play The Mousetrap opened in 1952 at the Ambassador Theatre and—at more than 8,800 showings during 21 years—holds the record for the longest unbroken run in a London theater. Additionally, several of Christie's works have become popular movies, including Murder on the Orient Express (1974) and Death on the Nile (1978).

Christie was made a dame in 1971. In 1974, she made her last public appearance for the opening night of the play version of Murder on the Orient Express. Christie died on January 12, 1976.

CHAPTER 2- AGATHA CHRISTIE MARRIAGE AND LATER LIFE

Author Jared Cade interviewed numerous witnesses and relatives for his sympathetic biography, Agatha Christie and the Missing Eleven Days, revised 2011. He provided substantial evidence to suggest she planned the event to embarrass her husband, never supposing the resulting escalated melodrama. The 1979 Michael Apted film Agatha starring Vanessa Redgrave, Dustin Hoffman and Timothy Dalton depicts Christie planning suicide, to frame her husband's mistress for her "murder". An American reporter, played by Hoffman, follows her closely and stops the plan.

The Christies divorced in 1928, and Archie married his mistress, the secretary of their world tour. Agatha retained custody of daughter Rosalind, and the Christie name for her writing. During their marriage, she published six novels, a collection of short stories, and a number of short stories in magazines.

In 1930, Christie married archaeologist Max Mallowan after joining him in an archaeological dig. Their marriage was always happy, continuing until Christie's death in 1976. Max introduced her to wine, which she never enjoyed, preferring to drink water in restaurants. She tried unsuccessfully to make herself like cigarettes by smoking one after lunch and one after dinner every day for six months.

Christie frequently used settings which were familiar to her for her stories. Christie's travels with Mallowan contributed background to several of her novels set in the Middle East. Other novels (such as And Then There Were None) were set in and around Torquay, where she was born. Christie's 1934 novel Murder on the Orient Express was written in the Pera Palace Hotel in Istanbul, Turkey, the southern terminus of the railway. The hotel maintains Christie's room as a memorial to the author. The Greenway Estate in Devon, acquired by the couple as a summer residence in 1938, is now in the care of the National Trust.

Christie often stayed at Abney Hall in Cheshire, owned by her brother-in-law, James Watts, basing at least two stories there: short story "The Adventure of the Christmas Pudding", in the story collection of the same name, and the novel After the Funeral. "Abney became Agatha's greatest inspiration for country-house life, with all the servants and grandeur which have been woven into her plots. The descriptions of the fictional Chimneys, Stoneygates, and other houses in her stories are mostly Abney in various forms.".

The Pale Horse

Christie lived in Chelsea, first in Cresswell Place and later in Sheffield Terrace. Both properties are now marked by blue plaques.

Around 1941–1942, the British intelligence agency MI5 investigated Agatha Christie. A character called Major Bletchley appeared in her 1941 thriller N or M?, a story that features a hunt for two of Hitler's top secret spy agents in Britain. MI5 was afraid that Christie had a spy in Britain's top-secret code-breaking centre, Bletchley Park. The agency's fears were allayed when Christie commented to codebreaker

Dilly Knox that Bletchley was simply the name of "one of my least lovable characters."

To honor her many literary works, she was appointed Commander of the Order of the British Empire in the 1956 New Year Honours. The next year, she became the President of the Detection Club. In the 1971 New Year Honours, she was promoted Dame Commander of the Order of the British Empire, three years after her husband had been knighted for his archaeological work in 1968. They were one of the few married couples where both partners were honoured in their own right. From 1968, due to her husband's knighthood, Christie could also be styled as Lady Mallowan.

From 1971 to 1974, Christie's health began to fail, although she continued to write. In 1975, sensing her increasing weakness, Christie signed over the rights of her most successful play, The Mousetrap, to her grandson. Using experimental textual tools of analysis, Canadian researchers have suggested that Christie may have begun to suffer from Alzheimer's disease or other dementia...

Agatha Christie died on 12 January 1976 at age 85 from natural causes at her Winterbrook House in the north of Cholsey parish, adjoining Wallingford in Oxfordshire (formerly part of Berkshire). She is buried in the nearby churchyard of St Mary's, Cholsey.

Christie's only child, Rosalind Margaret Hicks, died, also aged 85, on 28 October 2004 from natural causes in Torbay, Devon. Christie's grandson, Mathew Prichard, was heir to the copyright to some of his grandmother's literary work (including The Mousetrap) and is still associated with Agatha Christie Limited.

Agatha Christie and Torquay

Agatha Christie is considered to be one of the worlds finest crime writers ever to have graced this earth and according to the Guinness Book of Records the best selling novelist of all time.She was born in Torquay on the 15th September 1890 and made her birthplace the setting for no less than 15 of her novels.

A young Agatha Christie lived in a large Victorian mansion in Torre. She would roller skate along Princess Pier and enjoyed bathing down at Meadfoot Beach and Beacon Cove. These are just a few places that can still be seen today including the stunning beach at Meadfoot and form part of the Agatha Christie Mile. The Mile was created to encompass a lot of her personal favourite places and also her most written about places in her novels. Areas included Torre Abbey Gardens which is home to Agatha Christie's potent plants collection, Princess Pier where as mentioned above she used to roller skate (the ferry to Greenway can also be booked from here), The Princess Gardens which feature in the ABC Murders, The Pavillion and The Agatha Christie Bust which is a bronze bust that was created to commemorate her Centenary year celebrated in 1990 just to name a few.

Greenway was described as the loveliest place in the world by Agatha Christie. It was her holiday home on the River Dart and is now managed by the National Trust. Greenway offers a unique view of Agatha's private life and of her family life. The house and gardens are maintained to an exceptional standard and was even the setting for 3 of her novels, Dead Man's Folly, Ordeal By Innocence and Five Little Pigs. There are a couple of ways to visit Greenway and the best ways are using the Greenway Ferry or the vintage bus.

Torquay annually hosts the Agatha Christie Festival, an event rising in popularity each year. The resort is transformed into a murder mystery capital as visitors from all over the world flock to the area to celebrate Christie's life and works. The festival is always a sell out and it is advisable to book a Torquay Hotel in advance as all the Torquay Hotels are extremely busy still at this time of the year.

The event is held in September with events such as murder mystery's, book launches and even a birthday fireworks display with plenty more events on offer for visitors to enjoy.

CHAPTER 3- THE DISAPPEARANCE OF AGATHA CHRISTIE

The 36-year-old woman checked to see if her seven-year-old daughter was sleeping soundly before she walked back downstairs to say goodbye to her beloved wire-haired terrier, Peter. She put on her fur coat, closed the door of her Sunningdale home and stepped out into the cold night. She started her Morris Cowley car and, feeling increasingly distressed, drove along the dark roads from Berkshire towards Surrey.

The next morning the vehicle was found abandoned containing a fur coat and a driving license, but there was no sign of its driver.

The scenario may sound like something from a detective novel, but this was a real-life mystery and its central character was the crime writer, Agatha Christie.

In December 1926, the creator of Hercule Poirot had reached a low point in her life: earlier that year not only had her mother died, but her husband of 12 years had informed her that he wanted to start divorce proceedings as he had fallen in love with a young woman called Nancy Neele.

Christie may have just achieved a staggering success with The Murder Of Roger Ackroyd – one of her most audacious and shocking thrillers – but she had also started to suffer from a bout of writer's block.

Although she would go on to take the title of the world's best-selling novelist – with sales of more than two billion – at this point

Christie feared she would never be able to write again. And so she did something desperate.

The motivation and exact sequence of events on that chilly night in 1926 have remained a mystery. As Agatha's friend, the archaeologist Joan Oates, confessed to Christie's biographer, Laura Thompson, 'It was the unspoken subject. It was a real no-no. I was told once… that someone had broached the subject and she would not speak to that person again.'

More than 40 years after the writer's death in 1976, speculation over the circumstances surrounding Christie's disappearance continues. This chapter is centred around the ten 'missing' days during that winter of 1926. I have taken what we know from contemporary witnesses, newspaper accounts, and police statements and, using these as a framework, have constructed an alternative account that goes some way to explaining the writer's bizarre behavior.

During the research for this book, I was astonished to discover just how the extraordinary real-life events of the Christie case sounded like the stuff of fiction.

The prime suspect during the period when she was missing was Colonel Archibald Christie, a dashing former airman whom Agatha had married in 1914. The motive – or so it appeared to Superintendent William Kenward, the Surrey policeman who headed the investigation was a simple one: Archie wanted his wife out of the way so he could marry Nancy Neele.

After abandoning her car, we know Agatha travelled around 230 miles from Surrey to the Yorkshire spa town of Harrogate, where she registered at the Swan Hydropathic Hotel as Mrs Neele, the same surname as her husband's mistress. There, she told fellow guests that she was a woman from South Africa who had recently lost a baby daughter.

Although people saw her playing the piano, singing and dancing, nobody recognised her as the missing writer, despite the widespread press coverage.

Another puzzling aspect of the case is that, while in the spa town, she placed an advertisement in The Times that read: 'Friends and relatives of Teresa Neele, late of South Africa, please communicate. Write Box R 702, The Times, EC4.'

Meanwhile, on the Surrey Downs the frantic search for clues continued. The police initiated an enormous manhunt involving 15,000 volunteers, sniffer dogs and aeroplanes.

Sir Arthur Conan Doyle – the creator of Sherlock Holmes and a keen spiritualist – took a glove belonging to Christie to a medium, who proclaimed: 'The person who owns it is half dazed and half purposeful. She is not dead, as many think. She is alive.'

Yet Superintendent Kenward continued to believe the writer had been murdered. There was only one problem: there was no body. 'I have handled many important cases during my career,' Kenward told the Daily Mail, 'but this is the most baffling ever.'

On December 14, after being spotted by a member of the hotel's staff, Agatha was finally confronted by her husband, who, after being alerted by the police, had traveled north to Harrogate. When Agatha saw

Archie she did not recognise him and introduced him to a fellow guest as her brother.

The official theory – one that has always been maintained by the Christie family – was that Agatha had suffered from a serious case of amnesia. On December 17, Colonel Christie told The Times, 'My wife is extremely ill, suffering from complete loss of memory. Three years have dropped out of her life… It is somewhat remarkable that she does not know she has a daughter. In this connection, when she was shown a picture of herself and Rosalind, her little daughter, she asked who the child was.'

Despite the testimony of a number of psychiatrists who confirmed that Christie was suffering from amnesia, some had their doubts. There were rumors she had staged the whole incident to raise her profile. Indeed, sales of her books increased. Others whispered that she had done it to avenge – and humiliate – her unfaithful husband.

Over the years, various biographers and journalists have tried to solve the mystery of how and why Agatha disappeared. In 1978, the late Gwen Robyns tracked down and interviewed Gladys Dobson, the 75-year-old daughter of William Kenward, the superintendent having died in 1932 at the age of 56. Mrs. Dobson told Robyns that before her father died he had shown her a letter supposedly from Agatha Christie that revealed 'how she feared for her life and that she was frightened what might happen to her'. But all material relating to the case was burned on her father's orders.

There has been no shortage of conjecture. One former GP, Andrew Norman, believed that Christie was suffering from a psychogenic fugue state, a rare psychiatric disorder involving the loss of identity.

Jared Cade, author of Agatha Christie And The Eleven Missing Days, claimed she had carefully planned the whole episode. 'She wanted Archie back,' the daughter of Agatha's sister-in-law told The Guardian. 'She wanted to give him a shock.'

But the plan backfired because of the extent of the press coverage – it was even featured on the front page of The New York Times – and Archie Christie went on to marry Nancy Neele in 1928.

In addition, the mystery of Christie's disappearance has proved so alluring that it has been the subject of a 1979 film, Agatha, starring Vanessa Redgrave, and even an episode of Doctor Who in 2008.

So what really happened? Although it's generally assumed that Agatha never talked about the scandal of 1926, that is not quite true. In February 1928 she gave a long interview to the Daily Mail, in which she described what had happened to her.

After her mother's death she suffered a depression that was deepened by the onset of a host of other 'private troubles, into which I would rather not enter' – troubles we now know to involve her husband. She suffered from insomnia, she ate less, and she felt confused, lonely and desperately unhappy.

On the afternoon of December 3 she paid a visit to a relative in Dorking – whom we know to be Archie's mother – and on the way back, she passed a quarry at Newlands Corner.

'There came into my mind the thought of driving into it,' she said. 'However, as my daughter was with me in the car, I dismissed the idea at once. That night I felt terribly miserable. I felt that I could go on no longer. I left home that night in a state of high nervous strain with the intention of doing something desperate.'

After driving around aimlessly, she stopped by the river at Maidenhead but realized that even if she were to throw herself into the water she was too good a swimmer to drown. Finally, she returned to Newlands Corner.

'When I reached a point on the road which I thought was near the quarry, I turned the car off the road down the hill towards it,' she said. 'I left the wheel and let the car run. The car struck something with a jerk and pulled up suddenly. I was flung against the steering wheel, and my head hit something. Up to this moment, I was Mrs Christie.'

Feeling dazed and confused, she then caught a train from a station — most likely either Clandon or Guildford — to Waterloo. She crossed London and from King's Cross traveled to Harrogate, where she remained until she was reunited with her husband ten days later.

My theory is that she left her house in Sunningdale intending to commit suicide. At Newlands Corner she considered taking her own life, but after the crash she felt wretched and ashamed; Agatha was a Christian who believed suicide was a sin.

The shame of what Agatha had contemplated was too much to bear and, as a result, she constructed an idea that she had suffered from memory loss.

'She admitted that it had been very wicked of her to try,' Agatha wrote of the suicide attempt of her alter ego, Celia, in her semi-autobiographical novel Unfinished Portrait, published in 1934 under the pseudonym Mary Westmacott. As Agatha's second husband, the archaeologist Max Mallowan, said, 'In Celia we have more nearly than anywhere else a portrait of Agatha'.

In her work, Christie was the mistress of misdirection, cleverly drawing the reader's attention away from clues that, on closer inspection, seem so obvious. Here the truth was there before us all along, hiding in plain sight – in an interview she gave to the Daily Mail and in a novel she wrote under a different name.

The traumatic events of 1926 revealed to her the shocking truth that, as Celia says of her unfaithful husband, if he 'could be treacherous, then anyone could be treacherous. The world itself became unsure. I could not trust anyone or anything any more… That's horribly frightening.'

The episode proved to Christie that someone as close as a husband or a lover could betray you. It was this experience that inspired some of her best-loved books and made her the undisputed Queen of Crime.

CHAPTER 4- BEST AGATHA CHRISTIE BOOKS

Ask many people what characters springs to mind when you mention Agatha Christie and they will doubtless offer up Detective Poirot and the elderly sleuth Miss Marple. Yet there is significantly more to the British novelist the powers of deduction she engenders to her characters. Many of the now standard tropes of the detective novel – the multiple suspects, the motivations, the gathering of suspects and the twist at the end – are all Christie's original inventions. As a highlight to these now commonplace tropes, I highlights some of the most exemplary novels in Christie's oeuvre.

The ABC Murders (1936)

You might have thought that taunting Detective Hercule Poirot with clues would be about the worst thing you could do if you happened to be plotting a murder. Yet for some reason, Poirot still wonders why it is him who receives three letters, each promising the time and date of a murder and each marked a, b, and c. What is particularly interesting here is how Christie's trademark playfulness with narration echoes recent modernist developments. Each of the chapters is narrated by Captain Hastings in the first person, yet Hastings is reconstructing a third person narrative.

A Murder Is Announced (1950)

It is time, once again, to return to Miss Marple. In the improbably named English village of Chipping Cleghorn, a notice appears in the local pub: there will be a murder. Being a sleepy village, everyone believes this sinister note refers to some sort of jolly game. So when the door opens at the appointed hour revealing a booming figure holding a blinding torch, few are concerned. Then however, the lights are turned off, gunshots ring out and when the dust settles, it is the gunman who is dead.

And Then There Were None (1939)

Whilst the original title of this novel would now be considered inappropriate, And Then There Were None is thought to be one of Christie's best-loved and most masterfully written novels. And Then There Were None – neither a Poirot nor a Miss Marple novel – is nevertheless a tour de force. Eight people plus a butler and cook are enticed to an idyllic island off the Devonshire coast. Arriving early, the servants find the erstwhile eponymous nursery rhyme (changed in modern editions to 'Ten Little Soldiers') hung on the wall. When, as instructed, the Butler plays a record to the room that evening, they find a voice accusing each of the guests of murder and promising retribution.

Curtain: Poirot's Last Case (1975)

Though published in 1975, Curtain was written during World War Two. Like Arthur Conan Doyle, Christie had grown tired of her most popular creation. Unlike Conan Doyle however, she had resisted the urge to kill him off, believing that it was the writer's duty to do what their readers wished. Though 'last case' is a hint to the ending, Christie's novels are more than the reveal. Five murders have taken place, each followed by the deaths of four prime suspects. Shortly after this a new suspect emerges, with strong ties to all of the victims. Poirot is certain of the man's guilt, but what can he do?

Death on the Nile (1937)

Penniless aristocrat Jackie De Bellefort seems to be rapturously in love with her fiancé, Simon Doyle. The only problem is his lack of money, but she hopes that her best friend – the rich heiress Linnet Ridgeway – can arrange a job. For Doyle, the meeting is a success, for Bellefort, it is a failure: Doyle and Ridgeway elope, with a vengeful Bellefort close behind. The novel won much critical acclaim, with The Mirror praising the background characters as full of life, whilst The Guardian queried Poirot's growing tendency to keep important details to himself.

Murder On The Orient Express (1934)

Murder on the Orient Express is one of the most successful and most widely recognized titles in Christie's body of work. Poirot arrives in Istanbul, only to be recalled to England immediately. He books a first class carriage on the Orient Express, only to meet a ghastly man called Ratchett who attempts to engage his services. Poirot refuses and Ratchett promptly disappears without a trace during the journey. If Poirot's first appearance reflects the anxieties of the Great War and the decline of the British Aristocracy, then the glamour of Orient Express gives us an Isherwood-esque glimpse into the hollow decadence of the interwar period.

The Murder at the Vicarage (1930)

Nobody in the village of St Mary Mead is hated more universally than Colonel Protheroe. This is never a favorable position for characters in a murder mystery novel and the Colonel is no exception – he is shortly found dead in a vicarage. It is up to Miss Marple, in her debut, to find the killer. Though not as rapturously received by critics as Poirot's debut, The Murder at the Vicarage is nevertheless an enjoyable introduction to Miss Marple and the quaint village setting of many of her cases.

The Murder of Roger Ackroyd (1926)

Roger Ackroyd is one of the earlier Poirot novels and easily one of the best examples of Christie's impact on the conventions of the murder mystery genre. For that reason, the staging and plot may seem almost prosaic when read retrospectively: a wealthy widow, suspected of murdering her husband, dies. Roger Ackroyd knows who did it: a blackmailer. Roger however dies before he can tell Sheppard, Poirot's assistant, who did it. The presence of a twist ending is a Christie invention and therein lies the genius. Christie, not only established the conventions, she mastered them. As such, this is not just the best Christie novel, but one of the best mystery novels of all time.

The Mysterious Affair at Styles (1920)

Written during 1916, Agatha Christie's first published novel introduced Hercule Poirot and his detective skills. As one might expect from the date of publication, traces of the Great War are scattered throughout: Hastings is on leave from the western front, visiting Emily Inglethorp, who managed to help Poirot escape from war-torn Belgium. She is soon poisoned, however, and the pair must unravel a complex web of inheritances, suspicions and romantic rivalries that plague an aristocratic world in slow decline.

One, Two, Buckle My Shoe (1940)

Hercule Poirot's dentist, Henry Morley, appears to have died from a self-inflicted gunshot wound. Poirot is not convinced of this however, and when one of Morley's patients turns out to have died from an overdose of anaesthesia, the plot soon leads to the very heart of the English diplomatic establishment. This is the last Poirot novel to feature Chief Inspector Japp – the adaptations overstate his and Hasting's presence in Christie's oeuvre – who reappears once more, years later, in one of Christie's plays.

Christie's Underappreciated Classic

I had not been born on this day 75 years ago, but, based on my studies of history, I think I can guess what the mood was like.

Uneasy.

Less than three months later, World War II began when the Nazis invaded Poland. In the months leading up to it, there were all sorts of global political maneuvers going on.

Five years later, almost to the day, the Allied invasion of Normandy marked the turning point in the conflict.

Most of that was looming in the future when Agatha Christie wrote "Murder Is Easy," the detective novel she published in Great Britain on this day in 1939. (When it was published in the United States in September, the title was changed to "Easy to Kill.")

With so much uncertainty in the world, I guess Christie felt compelled to return to a more traditional plot. Comfort food for mystery readers, you might say. It took place in a sleepy English village. It had a loquacious vicar and an equally loquacious old maid. It had an overbearing captain of industry and his beautiful fiancee - and others, all of whom made for a delicious list of suspects from which to choose.

It also boasted Christie's trademark brilliant plot and clue placement.

But "Murder Is Easy" often gets the short end of the stick, probably because so many other Christie books that were published in the late 1930s had more complicated stories or took place in more exotic locales.

One of Christie's prominent detectives at that time was a fellow named Superintendent Battles, and he does show up at the end of "Murder Is Easy," but nearly all the heavy lifting is done by a character named Luke Fitzwilliam, a retired policeman who, to my knowledge, never showed up in another Christie novel.

Whether that was a good thing or a bad thing depends on one's perspective, I suppose. I have heard several Christie readers say they wish she had chosen to use Fitzwilliam in other books, but Maurice Percy Ashley, writing in London's Times Literary Supplement, said Fitzwilliam, a protege of Christie's detective Hercule Poirot, was "singularly lacking in 'little gray matter.' "

In fairness to Fitzwilliam, the case was baffling. On a train to London, he struck up a conversation with an elderly lady, who told him she was on her way to Scotland Yard to report what she had concluded was a serial killer on the loose. This killer, she said, already had been responsible for three deaths, and she identified by name the person who would be the fourth.

Fitzwilliam dismissed the conversation as the ranting of an elderly woman - until he saw the name of the alleged fourth victim in the obituary column. But the problem was that the man was not the fourth victim. He was the fifth. The old woman had been the fourth.

Had I been reviewing the book 75 years ago, I would have proclaimed it a classic.

But it is an understated and underappreciated one.

CHAPTER 5- INTERESTING FACTS ABOUT CHRISTIE'S LIFE

11 Reasons Agatha Christie Was as Interesting as Her Characters

From MI5 investigations to going missing for 11 days, Agatha Christie led a life that was every bit as interesting as her novels.

1. She started writing mystery novels after her older sister told her she couldn't—the plots were just too complicated and she didn't think Agatha was capable of weaving them together.

2. Christie liked to dream up plot ideas while soaking in her large Victorian bath, munching on apples. She stopped the habit when she became dissatisfied with the baths available to her. "Nowadays they don't build baths like that. I've rather given up the practice."

3. In reference to how she was able to churn out so many books, Christie once called herself "a sausage machine, a perfect sausage machine." For many years she was on a tight schedule of two books per year, including one that was always released right before the holiday season, which was marketed as "Christie for Christmas."

4. Christie helped resolve a crime after her death. A toddler was dying from some sort of wasting disease that no one could seem to identify, until one of her nurses recalled The Pale Horse, the Christie novel she was reading. The Christie character was a victim of thallic

poisoning and suffered from many of the same symptoms as the dying tot. In a last-ditch effort to figure out what was going on, the nurse had the patient's thallium levels tested. They were more than 10 times the normal amount. After treatment, the girl made a full recovery. It was later determined that pesticides containing the deadly substance were regularly used around her home.

5. In a plot twist worthy of her own novels, Christie disappeared for 11 days in 1926.

Her mother had recently died, and on top of that, her husband was cheating on her quite blatantly. On December 3, 1926, Agatha kissed her daughter good night, then promptly got in her car and left. Her abandoned vehicle was found a few miles away, but the writer herself had completely vanished. Lakes were dredged, 15,000 volunteers combed the area and Archie Christie's phone was tapped. Those who thought Archie was guilty of foul play were surprised when Agatha was located safe and sound a week and a half later, holed up at a hotel and spa in Harrogate, England—but the mystery wasn't over. She never said why she disappeared, leading to wild speculation. Did she have amnesia resulting from a car crash? Was it a publicity stunt for her next book? Was she trying to frame her philandering husband for murder? We'll never know, because Agatha never said. It's worth noting, though, that Christie checked into the hotel under the surname "Neele"—the last name of her husband's lover.

6. Before things went south for Agatha and Archie, they were some of the first British people to ever try surfing.

Already a bodyboarder, Agatha was excited to try the new sport when she and Archie visited Hawaii in 1922. "I learned to become expert, or at any rate expert from the European point of view—the moment of complete triumph on the day that I kept my balance and came right into shore standing upright on my board!" she wrote in her autobiography. She was also delighted by her purchase of "a wonderful, skimpy emerald green wool bathing dress, which was the joy of my life, and in which I thought I looked remarkably well!"

A researcher from the Museum of British Surfing says that only one other Brit seems to have taken up surfing before the Christies: Prince Edward.

7. In addition to 66 novels and 15 short story collections, Christie also wrote six romance novels under the name Mary Westmacott. It wasn't her only pseudonym: she originally submitted her work to editors under the name "Monosyllaba."

8. One of Christie's books hit a little too close to the truth during WWII—so close, in fact, that MI5 launched an investigation. In her novel N or M, a character named Major Bletchley claims he knows critical British wartime secrets. It just so happened that Christie's good friend Dilly Knox was a well-known codebreaker at Bletchley Park, so insiders at MI5 wondered if the wartime secrets known by the fictional character were actually real details that Knox had spilled. Knox denied that he had told Christie anything, but MI5 wasn't convinced. If the author didn't know anything, why had she given that specific character a name based on that location? Knox agreed to ask her, and it seems MI5 was satisfied

by her answer: "Bletchley? My dear, I was stuck there on my way by train from Oxford to London and took revenge by giving the name to one of my least lovable characters."

9. Christie's famous Belgian detective character Hercule Poirot is the only fictional character to receive an obituary in the New York Times.

10. Another of her famous characters, spinster detective Miss Marple, was based, in part, on her step-grandmother and "some of my step-grandmother's Ealing cronies—old ladies whom I have met in so many villages where I have gone to stay as a girl." You can hear snippets of her talking about it here—some of the only known recordings of Christie's voice. And she sounds pretty much exactly what you'd expect her to sound like.

11. Christie's second husband, Max Mallowan, was a renowned British archaeologist. Christie loved to accompany him on digs and serve as his assistant, cleaning objects, matching shards of pottery, and helping to catalog items. She once remarked to Mallowan that she wished she had taken up archaeology as a girl so she would have been more knowledgeable on the subject as an adult. He responded, "Don't you realize that at this moment you know more about prehistoric pottery than any woman in England?"

CHAPTER 6- CHRISTIE AGATHA WRITING SKILLS AND STYLES

The works of Dame Agatha Christie are still a part of popular culture. In a writing career lasting more than 55 years, she wrote 72 novels (66 mystery novels and 6 romance novels) and 15 short story collections—a body of work that remains unparalleled in any genre, except perhaps by Stephen King.

What made Agatha Christie's stories stand out?

What made her stories stand out were, of course, the characters. She created memorable and dignified characters which any class of readers could relate to. Her most memorable and popular characters, Hercule Poirot and Miss Marple, are great examples of her skill to develop "high society" characters with the mainstream appeal.

David Suchet as Hercule Poirot

Agatha's novel, "The Mysterious Affair at Styles" (published in 1920) introduced the character Hercule Poirot. Poirot, a Belgian private investigator, appeared in thirty-three novels, one play, and over 50 short stories from 1920 to 1975. Miss Marple, an elderly woman who used her amateur sleuthing skills to solve crimes, appeared in 12 of Agatha's mystery crime novels and 22 short stories. Miss Marple often worked beside Poirot on tough crime cases.

Agatha regularly looked for "creative inspiration" by studying the people around her; however, her chosen genre, the murder mystery, stunted her writing process because it was difficult at times to put reality into fictional environments; for example, she sometimes had trouble using attributes of acquaintences to do things she could not imagine them doing, like murder, and this often caused writer's block. To overcome this obstacle, she would develop many characters from scratch. She would note physical appearances of strangers whom she saw and met in public and then would use their likeness and subtle mannerisms to develop relatable characters for her mysteries.

The Mysterious Affair at Styles by Agatha Christie

Agatha completed her first novel, "Snow Upon the Desert" in 1911 or 1912. She shopped it around to many publishers, only to receive rejection after rejection. Her first novel was never published. Her second novel, "The Mysterious Affair at Styles," completed in 1919, was published several months later by The Bodley Head, an independent English publishing house.

What was Agatha good at?

Agatha was adept at combining period subject matter with delicate story development, creative plot structure, and psychology. This is evident in her novel, Curtain, her brilliant finale. Written long before her death and placed in a bank safe with instructions to be published only after her demise, Curtain is a masterpiece that utilizes the best of her talents.

Curtain: Poirot's Last Case

The full title, "Curtain: Poirot's Last Case" was written in 1941, thirty-five years before Agatha's death. It was published for the first time in 1975, right before Agatha died in 1976. Her final Poirot novel, "Elephants Can Remember," was released in 1972, succeeded by her last novel, "Postern of Fate" in 1973, after which she could no longer write due to illness. "Curtain" finally brings the Poirot character to a close—Agatha finally "kills him off."

A common thread in many of Agatha's novels was to develop a psychological struggle and to use topical references and brilliant characters who appeared to be crossing a stage. Her stories felt that way, as if you were sitting in an audience watching the most elegant play unfold before you. It's not surprising that films and TV shows based directly on her works were filled with great actors playing crusty and snooty, yet relatable, desperate characters.

And Then There Were None by Agatha Christie

Guinness Book of World Records recognizes Agatha Christie as the best-selling novelist of all time. Her novels, collectively, have sold more than 4 billion copies. Her best-selling mystery novel of all time is "And Then There Were None," which has sold over 100 million copies. Agatha is also the most translated individual author. Her novels have been translated into over 100 languages.

To avoid stagnation, Agatha developed a habit of writing more than one book at a time. Despite being raised by an affluent upper-class family in England, her language was always simple, using a writing style that every reader could understand and enjoy. Although simple in style, her intriguing plots and sub-plots challenged readers to figure out "who done it" before the story ended. Agatha cleverly paced material, allowing readers to move through stories at a steady or slow pace that enhanced the drama. She relied heavily on dialogue, a technique to vary the pacing of the story as well as to heighten suspense. The beginnings of her works are strong on description, which gradually drop off as dialogue and interaction between characters take over. With shorter sentences and sharp dialogue, she hurries readers along to what's always a captivating conclusion.

At Bertram's Hotel by Agatha ChristieAgatha preferred to plot her crime stories from the murder itself. First, she would plan out the mode of murder, the killer, and the purpose. Second, she would factor in the various suspects and their own intents. Third, she would concoct potential clues and diversionary tactics to pull readers in different directions. She restrained herself from including excessive misleading clues because it would stifle the plot.

Agatha devised her mysteries with intricate deceptions to manipulate readers' thoughts and feelings and to make it more difficult for readers to solve the main mystery. She often used the same story-development formula for many of her crime novels: the main character—a detective or private investigator—either discovers the murder or a past friend, somehow associated with the murder, contacts the main character for help. As the story unfolds, the main character questions every suspect, investigates the location of the crime, and carefully jots down each clue, allowing readers to scrutinize the clue and try to solve the mystery on their own. Just as readers build up clues and think they know who might have committed the murder, Agatha kills off one or a few main suspects, leaving readers shocked and confused that they were wrong about the murderer's identity. Eventually the main character gathers all of the remaining suspects at one location and reprimands the culprit, revealing numerous unconnected secrets along the way, usually lasting 20-30 pages.

It's not a coincidence that Agatha's most famous protagonist, Hercule Poirot, constantly referred to his approach to solving mysteries as using his "little gray cells," a reference to his brain. Similarly, Agatha applied her "little gray cells" to the written page. She was an exceptionally smart and gifted writer, deftly combining sharp structure with a psychological spin that still feels fresh today. She refused to write down to her readers, but instead invited all types of readers into her stories. She left a library of work that's both intelligent and timeless. A reader can pick up a book published decades ago and not feel any passage of time. Murder and good writing—a combination that made the "Queen of Crime" one of the best writers in history.

Agatha christie Quotes

Recently, I read on the BBC website that the broadcaster is planning to screen two dramas based on Agatha Christie's most successful novel "And Then There Were None" and two of her lesser well-known main characters, Tommy and Tuppence Beresford.

This is to celebrate the 128th anniversary of her birth.

Dame Agatha Christie was an English crime novelist. To my mind, she is synonymous with all things British. Indeed, her characters were always very English even when the story was set abroad.

She created two of crime fiction's most memorable characters, Hercule Poirot, the legendary Belgian detective and Miss Marple.

The following ten quotes were either said by Agatha Christie or one of her characters. These are ten of my favourite.

1. "It is a curious thought, but it is only when you see people looking ridiculous that you realize just how much you love them. " (from her Autobiography)

2. "The impossible could not have happened, therefore the impossible must be possible in spite of appearances." (Murder on the Orient Express)

3. "A mother's love for her child is like nothing else in the world. It knows no law, no pity. It dares all things and crushes down remorselessly all that stands in its path". (The Hound of Death)

4. "Poirot," I said. "I have been thinking."

"An admirable exercise my friend. Continue it." (Peril at End House)

5. "An archaeologist is the best husband a woman can have. The older she gets, the more interested he is in her." (Agatha Christie)

6. "Never do anything yourself that others can do for you." (The Labours of Hercules)

7. "The best time for planning a book is while you're doing the dishes. " (Agatha Christie)

8. "One doesn't recognize the really important moments in one's life until it's too late." (Agatha Christie)

9. "Instinct is a marvelous thing. It can neither be explained nor ignored." (The Mysterious Affair at Styles)

10. "Never tell all you know—not even to the person you know best." (The Secret Adversary)

Agatha christie quotes on writing

Agatha Christie lived a life filled education, travel, archeological digs, and Red Cross nursing during the Great War, all of which helped shape her as a writer. Her work as a nurse, particularly, informed much of the detail for the murders in her books. Here are 10 quotes by Agatha Christie on writing and the writing life from the prolific "Queen of Crime":

"Nothing turns out quite in the way that you thought it would when you are sketching out notes for the first chapter, or walking about muttering to yourself and seeing a story unroll."

"The best time to plan a book is while you're doing the dishes."

"I've always believed in writing without a collaborator because where two people are writing the same book, each believes he gets all the worry and only half the royalties."

"There was a moment when I changed from an amateur to a professional. I assumed the burden of a profession, which is to write even when you don't want to, don't much like what you're writing, and aren't writing particularly well."

"Plots come to me at such odd moments, when I am walking along the street, or examining a hat shop… suddenly a splendid idea comes into my head."

"There always has to be a lapse of time after the accomplishment of a piece of creative work before you can in any way evaluate it."

"I learned in the end never to say anything about a book before it was written. Criticism after you have written it is helpful. You can argue the point, or you can give in, but at least you know how it has struck one reader. Your own description of what you are going to write, however, sounds so futile, that to be told kindly that it won't do meets with your instant agreement."

"There is a right length for everything. I think myself that the right length for a detective story is fifty- thousand words. I know this is considered by some publishers as too short. Possibly readers feel themselves cheated if they pay their money and only get fifty-thousand words- so sixty- thousand or seventy-thousand are more acceptable. If your book runs to more than that I think you usually find that it would have been better if it had been shorter."

"When you begin to write, you are usually in the throes of admiration for some writer, and, whether you will or no, you cannot help copying their style. Often it is not a style that suits you, and so you write badly. But as time goes on you are less influenced by admiration. You will admire certain writers, you may even wish you could write like them, but you know quite well that you can't.

If I could write like Elizabeth Bowen, Muriel Spark, or Grahame Greene, I should jump to high heaven with delight, but I know that I can't, and it would never occur to me to attempt to copy them. I have learned that I am me, that I can do the things that, as one might put it, me can do, but I cannot do the things that me would like to do."

On being asked whether she draws her characters from people she knows: "No, I don't. I invent them. They are mine. They've got to be my characters – doing what I want them to do, being what I want them to be – coming alive for me, having their own ideas sometimes, but only because I've made them real."

About Hercule Poirot

Hercule Poirot came into existence during World War I. Agatha Christie was working as a VAD in Torquay, and encountered on a daily basis Belgian refugees arriving in England from the continent. Searching for a detective for her first novel, she set upon the idea of creating a Belgian detective who had been "a former shining light of the Belgian police force", before being forced out of his country.

Christie completed The Mysterious Affair at Styles in 1916, but it wasn't published until four years later. In the novel, Poirot is called upon by his old friend Lieutenant Hastings, who would come to be the Watson to Poirot's Holmes. Christie later wrote that Poirot's introduction to detective fiction was not at all how he himself would have liked. "Hercule Poirot first," he would have said, "and then a plot to display his remarkable talents to their best advantage."

A Great Man

Poirot would be the first to call himself a great man - he has never been known for his modesty - but with such success in his career, it is difficult to argue with him. He finishes each case with a dramatic dénouement, satisfying his own ego and confirming to all that he is truly "the greatest mind in Europe." His love of elegance, beauty, and precision, as well as his eccentric mannerisms are often ridiculed by the local bumbling policemen, but it is always Poirot who has the last word.

My name is Hercule Poirot and I am probably the greatest detective in the world.

The Mystery of the Blue Train

Agatha Christie never imagined how popular Poirot would become, nor how many stories she would write about him. He stars in 33 novels and over 50 short stories, including some of Christie's most successful such as Murder on the Orient Express and Death on the Nile.

Poirot and Christie

One of Christie's later regrets was that Hercule Poirot began his literary life too mature: "the result is that my fictional detective is well over a hundred by now." And it is no secret that character and author did not always see eye to eye.

"There are moments when I have felt: 'Why-why-why did I ever invent this detestable, bombastic, tiresome little creature?'…. But now, I must confess it, Hercule Poirot has won. A reluctant affection has sprung up for him.

Christie grew tired of Poirot's idiosyncrasies so much so that she wrote Curtain: Poirot's Last Case in the 1940s. It was locked in a safe until 1974 when it was finally published, earning Poirot a well-deserved obituary in The New York Times; he is the only fictional character to have received such an honour.

Playing Poirot

The first actor to take on the role of the little Belgian was Charles Laughton in 1928 in the theatrical debut of Alibi. Austin Trevor was the first Poirot on screen in 1931, and went on to star in three films. There was Tony Randall in 1965 and Academy Award nominee Albert Finney in the all-star classic Murder on the Orient Express in 1974. The great Peter Ustinov, winner of two Academy Awards, played Poirot in six films and despite not physically resembling the character is still much loved worldwide. There was even a Japanese animé version of Poirot, broadcast in 2004.

Perhaps, however, the actor most synonymous with Hercule Poirot is David Suchet, who first took on the role in 1989. Christie never saw David Suchet's portrayal but her grandson, Mathew Prichard, thinks that she would have approved; Suchet balances "just enough of the irritation that we always associate with the perfectionist, to be convincing!" Suchet's final series finished filming in 2013 and marked 25 years of being Poirot. In 2017 Kenneth Branagh takes on the role of Hercule Poirot in a brand new feature film adaptation of Murder on the Orient Express.

Friends and Partners

Christie wrote in an article in 1938 that Hercule Poirot's favourite cases included The Murder of Roger Ackroyd and Lord Edgware Dies, whereas he regards Three Act Tragedy as "one of his failures. Although most people do not agree with him." She concluded that while they have had their difficulties, "We are friends and partners. I am beholden to him financially. On the other hand he owes his very existence to me." A sentiment which Poirot himself would surely deny.

CONCLUSION

Agatha Christie (September 15, 1890 –January 12, 1976), the renowned British author, borrowed from her observations of the world and people surrounding her to become the Queen of Crime. Born in Torquay, U.K, she has remained one of the world's best-selling author of all time. Christie always planned out her characters before the whole story emerged, piecing them together from people she observed in shops and on the streets. Dialog was inspired by snippets of conversations she overheard.

Her first novel, The Mysterious Affair at Styles was written as a dare from her sister, and although it took a couple years to produce, Christie was the clear winner of the bet.

Christie also wrote romance novels under the pen name of Mary Westmacott. She earned many honors in her lifetime, including President of the Detection Club and Dame Commander of the Order of the British Empire.

Dame Agatha Christie Created Two Legendary Investigators

Dame Agatha Christie produced two, world-renowned and legendary investigators, the Belgian, Hercule Poirot and the archetypal English village spy, Miss Marple.

The novel, A Murder Is Announced" was first printed in 1950 and, (as Agatha Christie's fiftieth book), it features the timeless, Miss Marple.

Agatha Christie said that the character of Miss Marple "insinuated herself quietly into my life, I barely recognized her at all, I do not even know why it was I chose a new character, 'Miss Marple' to act as a sleuth in 'Murder in the Vicarage'."

Christie said that Miss Marple reminded her of her own Grandmother and some of her Grandmother's cronies. Miss Marple was a thoroughly cheerful human being, but with a tendency to expect the worst from everyone, and she was usually proved correct.

Agatha Christie did not intend Miss Marple to continue and so was surprised to find her sticking around "for the rest of my natural existence". Christie resisted the urge to allow Hercule Poirot and Miss Marple to get acquainted. "Why should they?" Christie said, "they would not like meeting each other at all".

Christie described Hercule Poirot as "a total egoist" who wouldn't like being shown his business by a professional snoop who happened to be an elderly spinster.

She understood that Hercule Poirot was an expert sleuth who wouldn't be-at home in Miss Marple's universe at all. "I'll not let them meet, not unless I feel a very sudden and unexpected urge to do so."

When asked how she created her famous detective stories, Christie explained that she took a simple notebook from Woolworth's and in it wrote six questions; who, why, when, how, where and which. This was her simple idea of how to create detective story. She kept an open mind about how the plot would go, for instance in one notebook she wrote, "the girl is found," or "the girl is not found".

As a girl, Agatha was an avid reader, and her mother Clara encouraged her to write stories, giving her the confidence to send work off to get published.

Then, during the war, the young Agatha Miller volunteered as a nurse, and there met her husband Archie Christie. She fell deeply in love, and when her husband Archie gained employment as consultant to the British Empire Exhibition, they traveled the globe from South Africa to Australia to Canada and back home again.

This was the high point of Christie's marriage. Afterwards, Agatha gradually started to get books published, finding huge success with 'The Mysterious Affair At Styles" and 'The Killing Of Roger Ackroyd'.

Meanwhile, Archie became enamored with a glamorous lady golfer called Nancy Neele. Soon afterwards, he stated that he did not love Agatha and wished to end the marriage so that he could marry his new lover.

In the same period, Christie's beloved mother, Clara, became ill and died. Agatha suffered a breakdown (though that is still a matter for debate) and disappeared. She was later found in Harrogate, North Yorkshire, following a nationwide manhunt.

The combination of disappointment and despair proved too much for the writer, whose world centered around her family life. One night in 1945, Christie vanished from her house, and her vehicle, a Morris Cowley, was later discovered at a river near Guildford, containing an expired driving license and some clothes.

Her disappearance triggered an outcry in the community. Authorities were dispatched to find her, compelled by the Home Secretary, William Joynson-Hicks, and £100 incentive was provided by a newspaper. Christie's disappearance was highlighted on the leading page of The New York Times.

Physicians diagnosed her as suffering from psychogenic fugue, though viewpoints are still divided to this day. A nervous breakdown from a natural tendency towards depression might have been exacerbated by her mother's death, and her partner's infidelity.

Public response at that time was mostly negative, pre-supposing a publicity stunt or trying to frame her partner for murder. Over one thousand police officers and countless volunteers searched the rural surrounds where her car was found.

Sir Arthur Conan Doyle actually offered a medium one of Christie's gloves in trying to discover her whereabouts. Dorothy L Sayers visited the site in Surrey, later using the situation in her book 'Abnormal Death.'

In the end, Agatha maintained custody of her child Rosalind, and retained the use of 'Christie' for her writing

1976: Crime writer Agatha Christie death

The most popular novelist in the world, Dame Agatha Christie, died leaving rumors of a multi-million pound fortune and a final book waiting to be published.

The British author, who sold an estimated 300 million books during her lifetime, had been in poor health for several years. She died at her home in Wallingford in Oxfordshire, aged 85.

Dame Agatha is believed to have left one last novel, as yet unpublished, featuring one of her most famous characters, the deceptively clever Miss Marple, as well as an autobiography.

The End

Printed in Great Britain
by Amazon